Scorpionfishes: Lionfishes & Much More for Marine Aquariums

Diversity, Selection & Care

Robert Fenner

Table of Contents

Introduction

Scorpionfishes are amongst the most readily recognizable marine denizens by aquarists and lay people alike. Many species are beautifully and cryptically marked and colored, and fancifully shaped. Bear in mind also that these fishes are mostly immobile, and often missed due to camouflage.

Some of the Lionfishes are amongst the most frequently kept marine aquarium specimens. Others, like the gorgeous Rhinopias species are greatly prized (and priced!) for their magnificence. Most all Scorpionfishes are feared for their spininess and venomous potential; and with good cause. These "Mail-Cheeked" fishes are well-suited for captive systems; shipping and adjusting well, accepting available types of foods, resisting disease and adapting to a wide range of water conditions.

However, of the some thirteen hundred twenty described species, the majority of Scorpaeniform fishes are unattractive; too drab and for their venomous nature best avoided by hobbyists.

Unknown by many aquarists is the full-spectrum of hardiness of this family of fishes; some quite hardy for our use; but how can you tell which species and individual specimens to avoid? Herein is my collection of first and second-hand observations on what the BFs are, where the species lie left or right of being generally hardy, and copious notes on how to pick out healthy specimens and maintain them.

There are literally Scorpionfishes for all marine systems; nano, fish-only of all dimensions to full-blown extra jumbo size reefs. Most are cryptic and retiring, sitting on or near the bottom, waiting for a meal to happen on by. Other than their spiky and venomous nature, the only other general downsides to keeping this Orders members is their capacity and willingness to suck down passing fish and sometimes crustacean tankmates. When considering a given specimen, do investigate the species capacity for growth, size in your system and select other biota accordingly. They are able to swallow surprisingly large tankmates.

Pertinent Biology & Husbandry Notes

Identification:

Classification: Order Scorpaeniformes, the "Mail-Cheeked Fishes", 25 families, about 166 genera, 1,271 species. There are a bunch of Scorpionfishes to put it mildly. All have large spiny heads, most with large eyes and mouths to match... for the most part sedentary to slow moving, stalking fishes... many are venomous... with hollow dorsal fin spines that can inject (with mechanical pressure) powerful proteinaceous toxin... These stings HURT; both mechanically and chemically. Here we'll list the more commonly encountered shallow marine species. The provisional higher taxonomic scheme is from Nelson mostly, 1994. Included are families and further detail below for groups that include aquarium species (there are several others).

Suborder Dactylopteroidei

Family Dactylopteridae, the Flying Gurnards. Two genera, about 7 species.

Suborder Scorpaenoidei. Contains world's most venomous fishes. Seven families, about 96 genera, 544 species.

Family Scorpaenidae, the Scorpionfishes, Lionfishes and Rockfishes. 56 plus genera and 388 spp.

Subfamily Pteroinae. The Lionfishes and Turkeyfishes

Subfamily Scorpaeninae, various Scorpionfishes, 15 plus genera with more than 150 species.

Blowin' in the Wind, The Leaf Scorpionfish, *Taenionotus triacanthus*

Subfamily Sebastinae, the Rockfishes. Important food fishes. Four genera, about 128 species.

Subfamily Tetraroginae; Waspfishes or Sailback Scorpionfishes, 11 plus genera and 35 species.

Subfamily Choridactyline (Inimicinae). Two genera, ten species.

Subfamily Synanceinae; the Stonefishes proper. Six genera, ten species.

Family Caracanthidae, Orbicular Velvetfishes. One genus, four species

Suborder Platycephaloidei, Crocodilefishes, Flatheads. Three families, 23 genera, about 75 species.

Family Platycephalidae, the Crocodilefishes or Flatheads. 18 genera of about 60 species.

Suborder Cottoidei, Sculpins; including "freshwater Lions", Lumpfishes; Eleven families; 137 genera, about 631 spp.

Family Cottidae, Sculpins; about 190 species

Family Cyclopteridae; Lumpfishes; about 28 species

Distribution: Scorpionfishes are found in all tropical to cooler seas, Atlantic, Indian and Pacific (though principally Indo-West Pacific) along rocky and coral reef shores. Most live in depths of less than twenty meters, though a few have been recorded to many times deeper.

Size: Most Scorpaeniform species as adults span about three to twelve inches total length; though some species exceed two feet.

Behavior:

Territoriality:

Scorpionfishes span the gamut of territorial behavior; some could care less; others react overtly to the presence of other species of fishes at times. Some "following" behavior is to be expected in predatory fishes, and there is often an apparent recognition of the aquarist... feeding-linked events, hand and arm in the tank while cleaning. The important issue here is to note that these fishes can be unpredictable in their tolerance of other biota; can and will lunge out and challenge others at times; with deadly result possibly. Best as always to not crowd these species; indeed, to make special efforts to assure they have their own physical space of use, and not co-stock other fishes and invertebrates that will either bother them unknowingly or seek to displace them environmentally.

Predator/Prey Relations:

Scorpionfishes spend most of their time at rest; though some families, notably the Lionfishes, have members that do get up and "go on the prowl" for food items. All Scorpaeniforms are easily classed as surprise predators, utilizing camouflage strategies in wait for organisms to ingest to happen by.

Here's an Antennata Lion out looking for some fodder. Lions and their kin hide out on the bottom, under overhangs, out of the way of current when water circulation is high. Come twilight and cessation of turbulence, you'll find them out searching; guiding fishes to eat with their over-large pectoral fins, at times hunting in con-specific groups.

Rapid and Repetitious Movement:

Dashing back and forth, up and down, even upside down at times by these fishes is indicative that "something" is off; usually water quality, though they can react overtly their own (internal; you may not be able to see it) reflection. If you encounter this behavior, it's best to thoroughly check your water with test gear, change out a good percentage even if nothing registers as off; and for reflection possibilities, cover over one or both ends (outside) of the tank with paper and tape.

Color Change:

Yes; Scorpionfishes do change color; more quickly, as in seconds to minutes, due to stress, mood and such; and more slowly; over days and weeks' time blending in with their environment. In fact, they can and do also grow and shorten "appendages", flaps of skin if you will, to blend in.

Shedding:

Sloughing off skin in mucusy strands is quite common in this group of fishes and is thought to aid in ridding themselves of external parasites.

Growth:

Mmm; yes; getting bigger (and shrinking) are behaviors; though longer-term ones. You should know that these fishes can grow rather rapidly; or not; depending mainly on what and how much, how often they are fed… up to, depending on species, a few to several inches in a year. Further you are cautioned to opt for slower growth; to extend your Scorpionfishes lives as well as prevent polluting your system. We'll have more to say in the later, successive section below on feeding.

Compatibility:

Scorpionfishes don't get along with all other potential fish and invertebrate livestock, and some, reciprocally, don't get along with them. As a general rule, any fish small enough to fit in their capacious maws (about half their length…) May well be inhaled; even if smart, fast, and living off the bottom. If you've been out diving or snorkeling at night, you are likely aware that many mid-water fishes make their way to the bottom to "rest" nocturnally. Many Scorpions are active at night; seeking such prey… And fishes aren't the only organisms at risk for becoming meals. Shrimps of all kinds, small-enough crabs, non-attached worms and even molluscs have been ingested in captivity. Other than small, mobile invertebrates Scorpionfishes are "reef safe"; that is; they won't eat your corals. However, they will "sit upon them", and though sedentary animals do produce copious wastes…

A list of anti-Scorpionfish fishes to beware of co-stocking is quite large; and though the likelihood of all not-getting along is not hard and fast; you'd do well to either avoid mixing these together or at the very least keep a close eye on the Scorps for signs of harassment, damage.

Some of the likely suspects in damaging Scorpionfishes: I'd skip mixing these together. Sharks, big Eels may try to eat them outright. Large Basses, Angels, Wrasses Puffers and Triggers, even Butterflies can pick them into stressful death. And do know that large crustaceans like big crabs and lobsters can work them woe as well.

Feeding Compatibility:

Another concern in arranging a stocking plan is making sure your Scorpionfish/es can compete for food with what else is in their system. Otherwise you'll need to stick-train your Scorps/s and use such a tool to deliver food items directly to them.

Human Concerns:

A note to urge your caution if and when moving, handling these fishes; and really, watching where they are whenever your body is in their system. All Scorpionfishes have spiky, spiny fin portions as part of the anterior of their unpaired fins… as well as spikey elements on their over-large heads. These REALLY hurt to get poked by; and you may suffer from a consequent bacterial infection from such an encounter.

And, if it hasn't been mentioned frequently enough, almost all Scorpaeniform fishes are venomous to varying degree; some potentially lethally so. Stings are delivered mechanically; that is, through pressure applied twixt the fish spine/s and the pushed against victim; forcing venom into the wound. These venoms are proteinaceous and of variable trouble in any given person… some folks being "more allergic" than others. They ARE painful to all however… and can be rendered less so via administering hot water to the wound site as soon as practical. HOWEVER, if you have a concern re an envenomation incident, I strongly encourage you to seek out medical care; and if in doubt, to contact the Dive Alert Network for assistance wherever you are.

Oh, and a personal comment re handling even dead specimens: Yes, they can still sting and poke you but good. Use a strong net with a good handle, NOT your bare hands in manipulating expired Scorpionfishes.

Selection/Stocking:

Species Matters:

You want to investigate before you buy any given species of Scorpionfish; some are much more likely to adapt, survive in captive settings than others. The Dwarf Lions; mostly of the genus Dendrochirus are exceptionally hardy, while others… don't make it very often. Further, some are more amenable to mixing with other Scorpaeniforms than others; some are rather social as the Dwarfs mentioned above; others best kept one to a tank.

Below under the coverage of the Order by Family and Subfamily, most often encountered species you'll find my statements more to these points. Suffice it to state that there is wide differential mortality in the group; and you want to be aware of your historical chances, and select for tougher ones.

Size Matters:

As with all livestocking, there is a too small, too large and about right range that is best to acquire these fishes. Too small ones ship poorly and are often starved; too big ones also suffer from the vagaries of collection and handling, and don't adapt well to captive conditions. A good general size range for the whole Order is 3-4 inches in overall length; hard to do with larger species like "the" Scorpions, Rhinopias, Stonefishes… but a goal to aim for.

Feeding Matters:

The "acid test" of proven feeding applies with these predators; and if your dealer has been utilizing freshwater fish, live or not as food, I'd leave them at the shop or put a deposit down and leave them for a week without these being offered. As you will come to know, a huge percentage of these fishes are lost to "gut blockage", "fatty degeneration" and other bad effects of being fed goldfish, rosy minnows and such. Ask to see your prospective purchase/s fed what you will be offering; and if they don't seem interested, neither should you be.

Damage Matters:

Of all fish groups, the Scorpionfishes rank supreme in terms of being able to recover from physical damage. I have literally seen finless specimens, ones missing a quarter or more of their body, recover completely. This being stated, I would still select for individuals that lack red marks, split fins; and that DO have clear, shiny and curious eyes.

Systems:

Concerning Size & Shape of the System:

The usual "as large as possible, practical" applies with keeping these animals. Yes; they're mostly sedentary, not moving around much or at all; but they are metabolically active, largish, messy feeders and waste makers; and need room to feel good psychologically. What is more; if you intend to keep other fish livestock, they will need/appreciate space to stay out of Scorpionfish territory. Even the smallest Dwarf Lionfish species should be kept in a 30-40 gallon system at minimum; the larger species require 75 plus gallons of uncrowded space per specimen.

About Décor:

Taking a look at the many images of these fishes and their natural habitats, what do you see? They are masters of disguise; hiding amongst rock, seaweed and more, blending in with their surroundings in shape, shade and color. You want to outfit their captive habitat the same; allowing your Scorpion/s to feel safely camouflaged; and further, to duck out of the light and principal currents.

Can you see the Scorpaenopsis in the pic at right?	

Leave some room around all edges, bommies of rock and coral work for them to get about; else you may find the rock toppled and your fish scarred.

About Circulation:

Depending on what else you have stocked, you'll want ten or more turn per hour of chaotic flow in the system (e.g. 1,000 gallons recirculated for a 100 gallon system); or even better, periods of circulation of higher and lower water movement that mimic natural tides and wave action (two higher, two lower per day or thereabouts). Dive-traveling aquarists will tell you that these fishes do move out of too-gyrating water during peak water movements; and out to feed and hunt at slack times.

To put this in another way; you want brisk water movement, but not continuous nor unidirectional. How best to achieve this? By way of multiple submersed pumps and/or power heads on a system of timers.

What Re Filtration:

A note of caution concerning powerful submerged pumps, powerheads, even some overflow discharges: these slow-moving fishes can become sucked up against intakes… DO screen these if using ones that are high suction.

Oversized and robust are keywords that describe the needs of filtration for these fishes. You want a doubled capacity skimmer, trebled biofiltration and daily removal/replacement, cleaning of mechanical filter media if you employ such.

Lighting: Very Important:

The intensity of light is a critical aspect determining these fishes health. A very large percentage of Scorpionfish die prematurely from too-bright settings; being blinded (though not the only cause; see Nutrition and Disease sections below); and overly stressed if not provided shaded areas to get out of light. Again; depending on your other livestock's needs, you want to have a shaded section of the tank for your Scorpionfish/es.

And these fishes are easily spooked by too sudden changes in lighting. Better to have outside light come on first and or have system lighting come on slowly (not abruptly).

Regarding Water Quality:

Scorpaeniform fishes are way off on the end of the scale in their resistance to "poor water quality" of most hobbyist types. They've even been used to "establish cycling" popularly in a few countries, spans of times. Understanding this, it is still a good idea to prevent their exposure to measurable ammonia and nitrite, and to keep nitrate below 20 ppm.

Some Scorpionfish species are euryhaline; that is, they readily adapt to different and varying specific gravity/salinity waters. Lionfishes notably are at times found in lagoons and river outfalls to the sea, living in brackish water.

Maintenance:

Frequent, regular water changes cannot be emphasized enough as safeguards of environmental viability. Ten-twenty percent a week, with pre-made, stored replacement water is my standard operating procedure.

Foods/Feeding/Nutrition:

Feeding Uninterested Scorpionfishes:

Is not a difficult proposition if you take your time. These fishes rarely starve to death; but do take a while to become familiar with captive conditions; unfamiliar foods. Best to use a "feeder stick", a wood or plastic dowel with a split or clip at the end to dangle food items just in front of the fish, slowing wagging it back and forth. Should the intended fish not respond no problem; remove all and try again tomorrow. IF your specimen goes without eating for more than a few weeks, shows signs of thinning, you may need to "stoop" to offer a live Damsel, brackish or marine live shrimp. See below re weaning onto non-live foods.

Oh, to mention them; there are two other quite common causes of these fishes going off-feed: Bullying by other fishes and aspects of poor water quality. For the former, the onus is upon you to closely observe your livestock… Angels, large wrasses, puffers and basses, and more will harass Scorpions to the point of causing their deaths at times. The presence of detectable ammonia, nitrite, more than 20 ppm of nitrate, metal-based and several "medicine" dyes among others will shift them to non-feeding. When, where in doubt, change some water out.

Hey Joe; Go Slow:

You want your fishes to be healthy, live long lives? Feed them sparingly and infrequently. Larger specimens can get by on twice, thrice weekly offerings; and never to satiation. Don't be fooled by how much they can jam down their throats; these fishes only eat every now and then in the wild. IF you go on holiday for a week or two; there is no problem with having them skip meals.

Beware Freshwater Feeders:

I so wish I had a dollar for every Lionfish and kin that is going to die today from being mis-fed "feeder" goldfish or other minnow species. Such "feeders" are a losing proposition for several reasons: First and foremost as mentioned they are relatively indigestible, and often the cause of "gut blockage" in Scorpaeniforms. Secondly; along with silversides, squid and krill-based diets they often lead to Thiaminase poisoning and deficiency syndromes that manifest themselves in blinding, malaise, going off-feed, and death. Thirdly, for what good they are, they're expensive and inconvenient to use. Lastly, there are some biological/pathogenic diseases that can be transmitted through their use. Instead you want to offer…. Marine foods.

Even Seawater Sourced Foods:

Thiaminase issues are a close second to freshwater feeder causes as sources of mortality. Krill and Silversides fed exclusively lead to this and avitaminoses deficiency syndromes and death. The best diet is one composed of a mix of marine based protein… a bag of seafood stew makings from grocery stores is the cheapest, simplest and most convenient way to nutrify your Scorpions… defrost and remove shells… wiggle on a feeding stick and Voila (!); you're done for a few days.

Yes; they can even be trained onto pelleted foods of high quality. Here is friend Pablo Tepoot feeding NLSpectrum to some Lions at his home in Homestead. Do you think the fish recognize the food container? You betcha.

Non-live food training requires patience and diligence. Healthy fishes of size can go without food for a few weeks… and you may find yourself tempted to "give in"; but don't! Mixing some dead meaty foods with what you intend to feed long-term is a good approach… shifting the percentages with time to your preferred items. Soaking foods mixed with HUFAs, Vitamins (Selco, Seachem Vitality…), and gut-loading live foods is a real plus.

Foods, Frequency/Amount:

Small species and specimens of Scorpionfishes are best fed 2-3 times a week; larger ones once or twice; BUT/AND never to satiation… Don't over-feed! Having the fish's stomach bulge out may appear funny, but is deleterious to its health. Better by far to actually not feed at all then to stuff them.

Disease/Health:

Scorpionfishes score about "middle" in terms of susceptibility to pathogenic disease; ahead of the curve in related nutritional troubles and are near last to succumb to environmental issues. Though relatively hardy then Scorpaeniforms do suffer from the same categorical ailments as all tropical marine fishes.

Diagnosis: The antithetical state of health that is disease can be detected via a few observable phenomena; and albeit these fishes are mainly sedentary, they do show signs of malaise, loss of equilibrium and outright damage. Careful observation and recording of routines like feeding and water quality tests will almost always avail in avoiding outright losses. That is, reacting in a timely fashion to identifiable behavior and markings can save your livestock in most cases. Look for split fins, haze in the eyes, excess mucus shedding, moping about and reaction to other livestock and foods as good clues that something/s may be amiss.

Environmental: Even though these fishes are tough, they are not immortal; and will succumb directly or not to environmental stress. Most issues are related to problems with metabolite accumulation, and are easily monitored via testing for aspects of nitrogenous cycling. The usual 0.0 readings for ammonia and nitrite and under 20 ppm (better less) for nitrate are de riguer. Frequent partial water changes (a fifth to a quarter per week) are the most sure, easiest means of assuring decent water quality; though some folks prefer the use of chemical filtrants like activated carbon et al. serving as adjuncts.

Difficulties with these fishes from system décor and pump intakes can be serious. You need to arrange hard-scape to allow them to be able to get around completely without getting stuck or scratched. Overhangs and caves must be provided so they feel secure and can get out of the bright light during the day. Strong intakes on pumps and overflows have to be screened to diffuse their suction; lest these fishes get sucked up and stuck on them.

Nutritional: We've covered these issues above under the "Feeding" section; but to repeat; MANY Scorpionfishes are killed off prematurely due to mis- and over-feeding. Beware of Thiaminase issues, gut blockage and fatty degeneration from the use of freshwater feeders; and be chary of proffering too much food too often.

Blindness in Scorpaeniforms is usually due to either too-intense lighting, or deficiency syndrome in foods. Do utilize useful food supplements; soaking foods ahead of offering. Blindness from either cause is reversible if caught, remedied in time; and even if blind they can be trained to take foods offered via a feeding stick. At right, a blinded Radiata Lion.

Trauma: These fishes frequently suffer from rough handling in collection, holding and transport; further from placement with incompatible tankmates. Starvation, ammonia burn in transit, biting by too-mean cohabitants can be remarkably overcome with basic quarantine under favorable conditions.

Social: We've gone over the principal issues of who gets along with whom generally under "Compatibility" above; know that Scorpaeniform fishes for their part typically get along with all fishes they can't ingest; but not vice versa. Eels, Basses, big Wrasses and Puffers, larger Angels and even some Butterflyfishes will pester them further than annoyance. All fishes and aquarists need to be cautious around the Scorpionfishes that are venomous, less they get poked or envenomized.

Scorps are "reef safe" other than inhaling shrimps and small crabs, but can be stung by Anemones; and cause water quality issues from their copious wastes; and may damage your benthic, sedentary livestock from settling on and amongst them too much.

Pathogenic Disease: Infections are secondary in almost all cases; as with other fish groups; the usual parasitic complaints (Crypt, Velvet….) occur and are brought on by stress and are best treated with Quinine Compounds.

Reproduction/Breeding:

Almost all species of Scorpaeniform fishes are unable to be distinguished externally as to gender; and those that have spawned in captivity have been almost entirely by accident. For those species on record egg masses are large, cohesive, released near the bottom from social and environmental cues; the young floating to become pelagic larvae of moderately long duration; settling down via chemical cues on shallow habitat. More coverage per group provided where known below.

Scorpionfishes, Order Scorpaeniformes; Aquarium Use* by Family & Subfamily

(*There are many more)

Family Dactylopteridae, the Flying Gurnards

Currently "darlings" of public aquarium display, Flying Gurnards are seen more and more as aquarium specimens. They are distributed in shallow, calm, sandy settings in the tropical Atlantic and Indo-Pacific, where they can be found walking on the bottom, hunting invertebrate food. Of note Flying Gurnards make noise by stridulating their hyomandibular bones. Some grow to more than 50 cm. (20 inches) in length; and all need large systems (hundreds of gallons) with plenty of open sandy bottom space.

Dactyloptena orientalis (Cuvier 1829), the Oriental Flying Gurnard. Indo-Pacific; Red Sea, East Africa to Hawai'i, Tuamotus, Marquesas. To 40 cm. Demersal; lives on shallow sandy bottoms. Only member of genus found on oceanic islands. N. Sulawesi image.

Dactylopterus volitans (Linnaeus 1758), the Flying Gurnard. Eastern and western Atlantic coasts. To ninety cm. total length (most much smaller). Feeds primarily on benthic crustaceans, especially crabs, clams and small fishes. Aquarium image.

Family Scorpaenidae: the Scorpionfishes, Lionfishes and Rockfishes

    Scorpion- or rockfish family Scorpaenidae ("Score-pea-nah-dee") are a group of fishes important to humans as food fishes and sources of envenomation (the subfamilies Synanceinae, the Stonefishes, and Pteroinae, the Lionfishes, among others). The non-toxic, but still very spiny rockfishes, in the genera *Sebastes,* and *Sebastolobus* are prominent table fare, sold as 'Pacific Snapper' in the U.S. though they are not in the snapper family, Lutjanidae. As Billy Shakespeare might say (or write) what's in a name. Sheesh. The family Scorpaenidae has widespread importance is reflected in its many colorful common names: Upside-Down Flying Cod, Butterfly Cod, Turkeyfish, Firefish, Scorpionfish, Zebrafish, Stonefish, and Rockfish, among many others.

Subfamily Pteroinae, the Lionfishes, Turkeyfishes

The marine aquarium hobby and service business would definitely be poorer were it not for the Lionfishes. They are the archetypal 'stock' captive fishes. Hardy, readily available, second only to damsels in accepting disastrous water conditions. Able to be trained to accept almost all types of foods and amongst the most disease resistant of specimens, lions are, would seem to be the best of captive aquatic life; and they are.

Except for the very real probability of getting stung by their venom bearing fins by being careless, the only downside of lionfish keeping lies in picking out healthy individuals, stocking with appropriate tankmates and not over-feeding them.

The subfamily Pteroinae, Aquarium Lionfishes: 5 Genera, 17 Species

For our purposes here let's limit the discussion to the Lionfish species important to the pet fish hobby and industry; that is, those of the genera *Pterois*, *Dendrochirus*, and *Brachypterus*. The first genus *Pterois* (Tare-oh-ease) are considered the "true" full-size lions, with huge pectoral fins, featuring unbranched rays with degrees of connecting membranes extending beyond the body at their insertion.

One Pterois and two other genera are more often sold as 'dwarf' lions. They display smaller, branched-ray pectoral fins with the rays sporting almost continuous membranes.

Also, a brief mention here regarding 'other Lion' species: There are several other genera in the Scorpaenid family offered from time to time as Lionfishes. For the most part these miscellaneous fishes are not as desirable as the species we will go over here. They are more secretive and far less appealing physically and color and pattern-wise. But, they probably are all venomous. Much more about this later, but it bears re, re, repeating: all Lionfishes are venomous and amazingly easy to get 'stuck' by. Yes, it's painful and may be very dangerous, especially if you have allergic reactions to proteinaceous stings.

And as regards the 'Freshwater Lionfish' sold in the trade; these are actually Sculpins, family Cottidae, related not too distantly to scorpaenids (in the same Order). For the record, besides not being Lionfishes, they are not venomous, or freshwater. There are some sort-of brackish water Scorpaeniform fishes, like the Bullrouts, that do make forays into fresh water, but they are not permanent residents.

The Lionfishes You'll Likely Encounter Include:

Pterois antennata (Bloch 1787), the Antennata Lion or Broad-Banded Firefish to science. This is the third lion confused with the volitans and Luna species. You won't make this mistake. Antennata lions have strikingly different pectoral fin rays. These are long, the thickness of pencil lead and bright white. Also, remember the connection, between the name Antennata for its relation to the black and white antennae (supraorbital flaps) and the six prominent spots on their face. To eight inches long. At right in Wakatobi, S. Sulawesi, Indo. Below: one in a typical day-time pose in S. Leyte, P.I.

Pterois miles (Bennett 1828), the Devil Firefish. Indian Ocean and Red Sea. Reddish, tan or grey in color. Note spots on median fins, numerous thin dark bars on head and body. To fourteen inches in length. An occasional import from the Red Sea, though more and more seen in the U.S due to its introduction into the tropical West Atlantic. Red Sea at right and an explant in St. Thomas, USVI below.

Pterois mombasae (Smith 1957), the Frillfin or Mombasa Lionfish. Alternating dark thin and broad body bars; spot on cheek. Indo-West Pacific; South Africa to Sri Lanka, New Guinea. To a bit over six inches in length. This one at Quality Marine in Los Angeles.

Pterois radiata Cuvier 1829, the Two-Bar Lion is the Radial Firefish. The most chameleonic of lions showing overtones of green, black and various shades of red over shocking white. The salient identifying characteristic of this species is the two while horizontal bars on the caudal peduncle, the part of the body right before the tail. At right and below Red Sea specimens. To nine inches in length.

Pterois volitans ("Tare-oh-ease vawl-it-tanz) (Linnaeus 1758), is the Lionfish to most folks. It is the most commonly displayed and sold member of the family; the quintessential marine aquarium specimen, with its long flowing pectoral and dorsal fin rays. Volitans lions span the color range of banded red to black against alternating creamy white. Yes, black and red volitans lions are the same species. Pacific Ocean; N. Australia, Japan, Marquesas, Australs... Replaced by P. miles in the Indian Ocean, Red Sea. Along w/ P. miles, an invasive introduction in the trop. W. Atlantic. A reddish one in Fiji at right and a blackish juvenile in Wakatobi, S. Sulawesi, Indo. Below.

Dwarf' Lionfishes in the genera *Pterois*, *Dendrochirus* ("Den-droh-kear-us) and *Brachypterus* ("Brack-ee-tear-oys") are labeled as such for their smaller size (up to about eight inches) and more sedentary, bottom-dwelling habits.

Dendrochirus barberi (Steindachner 1900), the Green (to the dive interest) or Hawaiian Lionfish. Eastern Central Pacific; Hawai'i and Johnston Atoll. Found in 1-50 meters of water, generally on coral or resting in rocky recesses. To about six inches total length. Very venomous to the touch. Here off of Kona, Hawai'i.

Dendrochirus biocellatus (Fowler 1928), the Two/Twin-Spot, Roo or Fu Man Chu Lion is unmistakable with its two eye spots on the rear dorsal fin area, and two whisker-like appendages extending from the lower jaw. To almost five inches in length. A wide-spread species found throughout the tropical Indian Ocean to the western Pacific, Mascarenes to Micronesia. At right, aquarium image, and one below in S. Sulawesi, Indo.

Dendrochirus brachypterus ("Brack-hip-tur-us") (Cuvier 1829), The Shortfin Dwarf Lion is a rarer, more heavy bodied dwarf, often showing up with a good deal of yellow, brown and green mixed with red markings. Brach dwarfs are aptly named in reference to their very large pectoral fins with almost no emerging ray tips. This is one of the most personable marine species, quickly getting to recognize and respond to its owner's presence. Indo-West Pacific; East Africa, Red Sea to southern Japan, Australia, Micronesia. Here in the Red Sea and N. Sulawesi, Indo.

Dendrochirus zebra (Cuvier 1829), the Zebra Turkeyfish, is the most common dwarf lion is similar in many ways and degrees to *P. antennata* and *P. sphex*. The one sure distinguishing mark of *D. zebra* is the presence of two white spheres on its caudal peduncle. To ten inches in length in the wild. Indo-West Pacific; Red Sea, East Africa, to Southern Japan, Australia. Shown: an individual in Sipadan, Malaysia at right and one in Bali, Indonesia below.

Pterois sphex Jordan & Evermann 1903, the endemic Hawaiian ("Dwarf") Lion; often mistakenly sold as Antennata lions which they closely resemble in terms of pectoral finnage. Sphex lion fins are shorter, less colorful and more clubbed in appearance. Though more costly than the majority of lions which are imported from the Philippines and Indonesia, Hawaiian lions are my favorite for hardiness. To eight inches.

And a Rare Species You Would Like to See:

Parapterois heterurus (Bleeker 1856), the Blackfoot Firefish. Indo-West Pacific; East Africa to Southern Japan. To eight inches in length. N. Sulawesi (Lembeh Strait) pic.

Dangers:

Are Lionfishes poisonous? Nope; in fact they're quite delicious, cooked or raw. Venom refers to materials that are toxic to the touch, poisoning generally comes about from ingestion. These fishes are indeed venomous, but they are not poisonous.

To illustrate this point, I was shocked one day while wholesale fish shopping with one of our aquarium service company's employees when he nonchalantly pulled a dying lionfish from a tank, pulled its skin off, tail to head, and promptly chewed the muscle off. Leif had been a Peace Corps volunteer in Samoa; helping folks there culture mussels for human consumption. He told me that Lionfishes are a delicacy there and offered to "peel me one". No thanks, but I have eaten the related California 'Sculpin', *Scorpaena guttata* which is actually a Rockfish (aren't common names exciting?)(Subfamily Scorpaeninae) cooked and sashimi and it is delicious.

Lionfishes are decidedly dangerous to handle, alive or not. I speak from painful direct and second-hand experience, having been stung myself a few times and been present when others have been.

Some people have been stuck when not exhibiting care while netting, moving a lion, dead or alive. Statistically though, more folks get poked enough while performing tank maintenance. Whether lions are truly aggressive toward humans appears to be a matter of debate amongst recent authors. It is not to me. I have been 'challenged' by head down, spine out lions while diving and as an aquarist. Whether it is out of food-response-conditioning, curiosity, territoriality reaction or what, Lionfishes will approach your arm when it's in the tank. They are unpredictable. You want to have one eye on your Lion(s) and one on the task at hand anytime you're in the system.

Eleven to thirteen dorsal spines, three anal spines and two pelvic fin spines sheath a glandular complex some two-thirds their length along anterolateral grooves. Venom passes through mechanical means, unlike the pumping action of the Stonefishes, you and the lion jamming against each other. Though not as toxic as their stonefish cousins, lion stings must be taken seriously. Swelling, soreness, localized pain, respiratory and cardiac distress, and other collateral shock manifestations go with these events. Ringing your local Poison Center, and immersing the area of entry site with water as hot as you can tolerate are immediately called for.

Natural and Introduced Range:

Found naturally in tropical Pacific and Red Sea rocky reefs, ten to two hundred feet of depth; introduced to western Atlantic, Carolinas to Brazil and Gulf of Mexico.

Size:

Most *Pterois* grow to about a foot and a half in the wild (half this in captivity), the dwarf genera to approximately six inches total length in captivity.

Selection:

For the most part Lionfishes are easily captured (they don't swim quickly, are easily found in the wild), but they do take a beating in transit, holding, transit... on their way to your dealers. For girthy fishes with sizable appetites they are rather sensitive to ammonia poisoning and low oxygen concentration... Hence:

1) **Don't buy newly arrived specimens**... Let the poor fish rest up from being collected (all are wild-captured) for a few days to a week. Most all "anomalous losses" of these fishes occurs within a few days of collection and transport.

2). **Don't purchase "spaced out" individuals**. Healthy specimens are bright-eyed, alert, aware of your presence, not cowering in the corner or with cloudy eyes.

3) **Avoid specimens with red markings or open sores**. Torn fins are fine and will mend... they get broken in collection, being shipped in poor quality water, and the food-less interval of days to weeks before your shop's acquiring them... But look out for bad scrapes, and infected lateral lines. Look particularly at the fin insertion areas of the body for tears, evidence of bleeding. Most damaged individuals will heal, but its best that they are not moved about when they are so impugned.

4) Hold off on purchasing fishes that don't eat at your dealers. This "old saw" is a valid yes/no decision maker for purchasing lions. A healthy lionfish will always show interest... at least awareness of potential food items in its vicinity. If one that you have your eye on won't take food in front of you, put it on "layaway" with a deposit and come back for it... feeding, at a later date.

Collecting Your Own: You can gather your own if you happen to be in their distribution/area: Lionfishes evidently consider themselves top reef dogs. Best time to net them, right out of the open water, is between sun ups and downs. During the day look in nooks and crannies for *Pterois* and under rock and rubble (I'm serious) for 'dwarf species'. The usual malarkey here for permits and capture and transport paraphernalia.

Environmental: Conditions

Other than overfeeding with too much, too soon goldfish, this is the second deadly area where aquarists fail with their lions. Lionfishes, for all their apparent slow-moving, calm breathing, seemingly low metabolic lifestyles need space; room to move, sites to hide/feel comfortable in, volume of water to provide adequate oxygen, dilution of their, at times, copious wastes.

Habitat:

Lionfish systems need to be large; bigger, the better; a good 30-40 gallons minimum per adult *Pterois* and half that for other species.

Chemical/Physical:

Though lions don't appreciate fast swings in temperature, they have enormous range tolerance. I have 'found' them in forgotten tanks at wholesalers in incredibly saline water, so much they should have been floating on top.

A super-commonplace problem with 'lion tanks' is the loss of alkaline reserve with over feeding, inadequate filtration, infrequent water changes. The scenario goes like this. Owner/keeper wants to impress most anyone and gorges lionfishes at every opportunity. Water quality tanks, with pH diving dangerously below 7.6, lions go into hiding, breathing heavily. Owner calls their service company complaining. Service personnel either 1) get there quick, make massive water change and/or add buffering agent to system, or 2) get there too late with tank turning to bouillabaisse. Lesson to be learned here: keep guard on at least pH; do frequent large % water changes.

Filtration:

These fishes filtration needs be capable of handling occasional large amounts of solid waste and efficient to keep ammonia and nitrites unmeasurable. In the ancient days of marine aquarium keeping some writers advocated using lions instead of damsels for establishing nutrient cycling; but they assuredly suffer from exposure to nitrogenous wastes.

Display:

Provide open and closed spaces, such as lions utilize in the wild. They hide during brightest day; yours will too. This leads us to, tah-dah, and lighting. Make it subdued, low illumination fluorescents, at least a dark corner. Glaring lights are implicated in lion "blindness" environmental disease. Note the opacity in this Radiata eye from being kept in too bright a system.

Behavior:

Territoriality:

No overt negative behavior toward other livestock of size generally. Lions are very willing to share living space with their own and other lionfish species. They are celebratedly known to cooperate in feeding/herding behavior in the wild.

Introduction/Acclimation

Very simple for local purchase (versus long hauls); adjust for temperature and release.

Predator/Prey Relations:

Very easygoing with anything they can't inhale; but they do have very large, distensible mouths. Damsels, etc., and non-attached invertebrates are all so much aqua-popcorn, and should be anticipated to be ultimately sucked in. The typical 'wise-guys', triggers, puffers, large angels... you'll have to keep an eye on these so they don't hassle your lion(s).

Reproduction, Sexual Differentiation/Growing Your Own:

There are a few accounts (German and other mid-European) of captive, as in public aquaria, spawnings. Some scorpaenids are known to be ovoviviparous, a form of live-bearing, but *Pterois* are surface egg scatterers. Near artificial dusk, a male and female engage in a simple pre-spawning 'dance' culminating in upward swimming and simultaneous release of gametes while upside down beneath the surface. No record of eggs hatched and reared.

Feeding/Foods/Nutrition: Types, Frequency, Amount, Wastes

Quick! What's the number one cause of death of captive Lionfishes? Here's a little clue; what section are you reading: Foods and feeding. If food is love than most lions are loved to death. Postmortem exams we've done invariably show fatty liver degeneration (yellow, floating blobs), frequently with accessory gut impaction from, and guess what? Excessive Feeder Goldfish Gobbling Syndrome.

Open wide! This "smiling" Lionfish image belies just how large an object (sometimes inanimate) that Lions and relatives can ingest! Take care to have only "larger than mouth-size" tankmates.

Here's how it works: "Check it out, Uncle Al; this here Turkeyfish can swallow a dozen of these golden beauties at a throw, Oooowhee." Don't do it! To yourself, your Lion(s), or 'feeders'! Goldfish are not a good steady diet for several reasons. They're nutritionally deficient, inconvenient, expensive.... and may make your Lion(s) aggressive. And furthermore, they're unnecessary. Lionfishes can and should be trained to accept better foods. Frozen, fresh, prepared types of all kinds; silversides, krill, shrimp, crabs, crickets... avoid oily, greasy foods, including feeders. See my whole take on: Feeding Feeders.

Notes on food training: Using a feeding stick/rod, move the offered food in front of the lion; if not accepted, remove for another day. Not to worry if your charge goes on a food strike of a few to several days. If in good health, this presents no problem, and is a useful technique for limiting growth. A new specimen that refuses dead food may need to be weaned with live first. Try guppies or a live shrimp or crab placed ahead of the lion.

Remember, the principal cause of Lion death is over-stuffing. Do Not Overfeed. Depending on livestock and food size, desired growth rate, feed once, twice or three times a week maximum; keep them hungry.

Disease: Infectious, Parasitic, Nutritional, Genetic, and Social

Lionfish acquisition, preventative treatment and introduction conform to the suggested 'Brand X' path as for most marines: 1) Quarantine for two weeks, or at least 2) Run through a freshwater, and/or marine/dilute formalin bath to reduce external parasite introduction.

Fin rot due to mis, over-handling in shipment is easily cured with furan compounds in the trade. The common protozoal scourges *(Amyl)Oodinium, Brooklynella and Cryptocaryon* clear up easily with copper sulfate treatment or Quinine compound administration, if caught/observed in time.

Shedding of skin is something you will experience with lionfishes. Related coughing, shaking et al. may accompany it. In related species this activity is thought to aid in ridding of algae growth on camouflaging skin flaps, parasites... Once again, try not to worry.

Close:

So what have you learned from all this? That it is my opinion that lionfishes make great pet-fishes so long as you 1) are aware that they're venomous and accordingly keep your distance. 2) That they're practically indestructible, except for overfeeding, particularly with 'feeder goldfish' and 3) Water quality degradation due to number 2), overcrowding and/or inadequate filtration. Good.

Further Reading:

USGS report on invasive species; P. volitans:
Schofield, PJ, JA Morris, Jr, JN Langston, and PL Fuller. 2014. *Pterois volitans/miles*. USGS Nonindigenous Aquatic Species Database, Gainesville, FL.
http://nas.er.usgs.gov/queries/factsheet.aspx?speciesid=963 Revision Date: 9/18/2012

Campbell, Douglas. 1984. *Pterois volitans*. FAMA 9/88.

Emmens, C. W. 1983. Spotlight: Lionfishes. TFH 4/83.

Fenner, Robert. 1993. An Argument Against "Feeder" Goldfish. FAMA 11/93.

Kendall, J.J. 1990. Further evidence of cooperative foraging by the Turkeyfish, *Pterois miles* in the Gulf of Aqaba, Red Sea with comments on safety and first aid. Diving for Science 1990. Proceedings of the American Academy of Underwater Sciences Tenth Annual Scientific Diving Symposium, Oct. 4-7, 1990. Univ. of S. Fla., St. Petersburg. pp. 209-223.

Kizer, Kenneth W., Howard McKinney and Paul S Averbach. 1985. Scorpaenidae envenomation: A five year poison center experience. TFH 7/85.

Mayland, Hans J. 1975. Lionfish, beautiful but dangerous. Marine Aquarist 6(2):75.

Modlin, Jon R. 1982. The Lion Tree. FAMA 3/82.

Nelson, Joseph S. 1994. Fishes of the World, 3rd ed. John Wiley & Sons, the World.

Romaine, Deborah S. 1978. The Lionfish: Mr. Personality. TFH 5/78.

Walker, Stephen D. 1984. *Pterois radiata*, the fireworks fish. FAMA 8/84.

Subfamily Sebastinae, the Rockfishes.

Mainly as important food and game fishes; Rockfishes are often mis-labeled as "Snappers" off the US west coast (we have no true snappers, Family Lutjanidae). You may well find some of these species lolling about in public aquariums; as they are handsome and hardy. Four genera, about 128 species.

Genus Sebastes:

Sebastes paucispinis Ayres 1854 The Bocaccio. A favored rockfish for human consumption. Found off the west coast of the U.S.; Baja to Alaska. Here, a juvenile and small sub-adult at SIO Birch Aq.

Subfamily Scorpaeninae, various Scorpionfishes

Genus Iracundus: Monotypic.

Iracundus signifer Jordan & Evermann 1903, the Decoy Scorpionfish. Has a marking above the largely transparent base of the anterior dorsal fin that resembles a small fish... that this species undulates as a lure. Indo-Pacific near the ends of reef slopes on sand and ledges. To five inches long. Hawai'i image.

Genus Parascorpaena: Seven species.

Parascorpaena picta (Cuvier 1829), the Northern Scorpionfish. Indo-West Pacific. To 16 cm. in length. N. Sulawesi specimen.

Genus Pteroidichthys: Two species.

Pteroidichthys amboinensis Bleeker 1856, the Ambon or Hairy Scorpionfish. To about four inches in length. West Pacific. Here in N. Sulawesi (Lembeh Strait)

Genus Rhinopias:

Rhinopias aphanes Eschmeyer 1973, Merlet's Scorpionfish. Indo-Western Pacific; northern Australia, New Guinea, southern Japan. To 25 cm. in length. A rare species that lives at the bottom of coral slopes or on soft bottoms. Phil Sokol image in Papua New Guinea.

Rhinopias aphanes Eschmeyer 1973, Merlet's Scorpionfish. . Indo-West Pacific. To about 17 cm. Aquarium image.

Rhinopias frondosa (Gunther 1892), the Weedy Scorpionfish. Indo-Western Pacific; East coast of Africa to the Carolines, southern Japan. To 23 cm. in length. Aq. pic.

Genus Scorpaena

Scorpaena mystes Jordan & Starks 1895, the Pacific Spotted Scorpionfish. To eighteen inches in length. Eastern Pacific: Sea of Cortez to Peru, including the Galapagos. Found sitting on sandy and rocky bottoms surface to 25 meters of depth. Galapagos pix.

Scorpaena plumieri Bloch 1769, the Spotted Scorpionfish. To eighteen inches in length. Western Atlantic: Massachusetts, northern Gulf of Mexico to southern Brazil, Ascension and St. Helena. Found sitting on rocky bottoms 5-55 meters of depth... ambushing fishes and crustaceans for food. Occasionally imported as an aquarium species. Key Largo pic.

Genus Scorpaenodes:

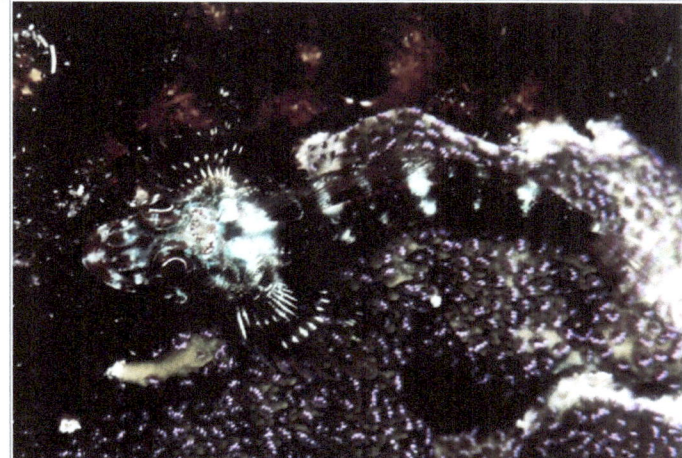

Scorpaenodes littoralis (Tanaka 1917), the Shore Scorpionfish. Indo-Pacific on reefs, or rocky bottoms. To 11 cm. This one off of the Whitsundays, Queensland, Australia.

Scorpaenodes parvipinnis (Garrett 1864), Lowfin Scorpionfish. To 14 cm. Indo-Pacific; Red Sea to Tuamotus, Hawai'i. Found in areas of rich coral growth. Cryptic, reclusive by day. N. Sulawesi pic.

Genus Scorpaenopsis:

Scorpaenopsis barbata, Red Sea

Scorpaenopsis cacopsis Jenkins 1901, Titan Scorpionfish. Long third dorsal spine. Hawaiian island endemic. Due to its high regard as a food fish, its populations have been decimated by spearfishers. To twenty inches long. Big Island pix.

Scorpaenopsis diabolus (Cuvier 1829), the False Scorpionfish. Indo-Pacific; Red Sea to Hawai'i, Micronesia, Australia. To 30cm. Right, in Hawai'i. Below: N. Sulawesi images.

Scorpaenopsis oxycephala, the Tasseled Scorpionfish Have prominent tassels of skin on lower head. Adults lack cirri around eyes

Scorpaenopsis papuensis (Cuvier 1829), Papuan Scorpionfish. To ten inches in length. Indo-pan Pacific. Adult in Fiji.

Scorpaenopsis possi, Poss's Scorpionfish. Of the genus has a short snout, fewer pectoral fin rays (17 vs. 19, 20). Small or absent eye cirri. Red Sea, E. Africa to Polynesia, Australia and ROC.

Scorpaenopsis venosa (Cuvier 1829), the Raggy Scorpionfish. Indo-West Pacific; East Africa to the Philippines, down to Australia. To a foot in length. Often found lying on top of soft corals and sponges, disguised waiting for a meal to come by. Shown here in N. Sulawesi, Indonesia.

Genus Taenionotus: The Leaffish. Such an outstanding species for aquarium use that we'll dedicate a few pages to its coverage:

Blowin' in the Wind, The Leaf Scorpionfish, *Taenionotus triacanthus*

Taenianotus triacanthus Lacepede 1802, the Leaf Scorpionfish. Indo-pan-Pacific. To four inches overall length. Usually found amongst reef rocks on an open setting, rocking like a falling leaf. Molts twice a month. Feeds on small fishes, fry and crustaceans. Comes in browns, blacks, yellows, reds. At right, in Hawai'i. Below, first row, an assortment in N. Sulawesi. Second row in Gili Air, Indonesia, light purple! Second also off Gili Air, the last in Fiji. Third, N. & S. Sulawesi,

The Lionfishes that hobbyists are familiar with are just the beginning of a vast assemblage of "Mail-cheeked fishes" that comprise the Order Scorpaeniformes... 25 families, about 166 genera, 1,271 species. There are "a bunch" of "Scorpionfishes" to put it mildly. All have large heads, most with large eyes and mouths to match... for the most part sedentary to slow moving, stalking fishes... many are venomous... with hollow dorsal fin spines that can inject (with mechanical pressure) powerful proteinaceous toxin... These stings can hurt you mechanically and chemically, and must therefore be handled with care.

Our species of interest here sides far on the mild side of the scale in terms of danger... Unlike the common Pteroine Lions that do a good deal of stalking of prey, and at times present their hypodermic fin spines at aquarists, Taenionotus triacanthus prefers to "sit about" in disguise, waiting for a meal to happen by... About the most outgoing reaction one gets from them is yawning and gentle side to side motion... like, you guessed it, a leaf.

The Leaf Scorpionfish is monotypic... that is, it is the sole member of its genus... Of the largest subfamily (Scorpaeninae) of Rock and Scorpion fishes (Scorpaenidae)... This group of mail-cheeked fishes alone has some 15 genera and more than 150 species. Some notable species here include the Gorgeous genus Rhinopias, Ambon or Hairy Scorpionfish (*Pteroidichthys amboinensis*), and the largish Scorpionfishes of the genus Scorpaena.

An assortment of colors and markings for Taenionotus triacanthus. Not only variable, but change-able, mostly dependent on surroundings they can change to match and hide within their environment.

Selection:

Finding actual specimens of these species is the hard part of selection... It's never super-abundant in the wild, and not easily found to boot. Ones that do make their way into the trade are almost always "ready to go" in terms of their health and lack of damage from collection, holding and shipping. Happily this IS a very inactive species... that DOES virtually scoot around on its stocky pectoral fins... Such traits blend well with being "quiet" in small volumes, like holding tanks, fish bags... and not puncturing these last or breaking fin spines like their more "turkey" brethren.

Do the usual wait for a few days on newly-arrived specimens... Most that will die mysteriously do so within a night or two... If you're concerned re someone else buying a prospective specimen, do put down a deposit and have the store label the tank it is in for your reservation.

Compatibility:

As with their larger kin, the Lionfishes, Leafs get along pretty much with everything that gets along with them... The usual exceptions include outright territorially aggressive species like many Triggerfishes, large and small-nippy Puffers, larger Wrasses... and small-enough-to fit in their mouths fish groups like Damsels, Grammas, Dottybacks and such. Also to be aware of are avoiding animals that will too-easily outcompete your Leaf for food... Once the item is within striking distance, this species can move/inhale prey lightning fast... but other fishes (e.g. Hawks) may well collect all offered food before it gets that far. We're talking peaceful, not too-frisky fish tankmates here, like Dart Gobies, Anthiines...

Can you have more than one? Yes... this species is often encountered in the wild in "pairs", sometimes with quite a few more individuals scattered about. There are some apparently agonistic/territorial Scorpaeniform fishes... in the wild and captivity; but this is not one of them. If you have room for perches, adequate filtration, more than one specimen can be maintained in a given system.

Concerning Invertebrates; for completeness sake I will mention that there is the occasional transgression with purposefully placed small shrimps and even Hermit Crabs being consumed... but as far as most sessile and motile invertebrates go, they are very safe with this Scorpaenid. In fact, you're encouraged to have an assortment of well-established corals (hard and/or soft), other Cnidarians that are getting along, any other Phylum of non-vertebrate animal, plus living macroalgae in with your Leaf. See the accompanying images here? This fish is found nestled amongst other living reef inhabitants... and can/will grow dermal appendages, change color to match what you provide... Make it diverse.

Oh, and yes, *Taenionotus triacanthus* does have/bear venomous spines... so do take care if/when you are netting this fish, to keep your hands away or something substantial in-between you and the net.

Systems:

Folks seem to consider that if an animal is rather sedentary that it doesn't need much space to live... well. This is assuredly not the case, with even almost-permanently ensconced fish like the Leaf Scorpion requiring a good volume of water for psychological purposes as well as dilution of wastes, surface area for gas exchange... and room for your creative habitat designing! At a minimum, I would use nothing smaller than a 29 gallon tank for one specimen and more than these three dimensions if you intend to keep much with it.

Regarding water quality, I'd like to see the same sort that you would apply and be diligent re maintaining... for a typical reef system; lots of healthy, established live rock etc. After all, this is exactly where this species occurs. Though most folks think they're providing a good deal of water circulation, a brief trip to a natural reef surprises most all... Any given volume of water is traded out per minute at what the majority of aquariums move per hour... Don't be concerned re having too much current with Leaffishes... if it's too brisk or uni-directional, this will show in the animal's behavior... Moving to a spot or spots where it feels most comfortable.

Foods/Feeding:

Initially you may well have to feed your new Leaffish live food... gut-loaded (Cyclop-eeze and soaked in vitamin/HUFA prep. like Selcon) ghost shrimp are great here, and generally available. Over time frozen/defrosted foods will generally become accepted with training (a "feeding stick"... wood or plastic dowel...) For small specimens frozen Mysis are excellent here, as are most any sea-origin meaty item that doesn't have much shell.   It is advised that you only feed about once, maybe twice a week. You want your Leaf (actually all fishes) to not be too plump in their belly-region, but not concave either.

Disease:

Scorpaeniform fishes look rough and tough, but when it comes to chemical exposure they can be quite dainty. If possible, avoid exposure at high strength with copper compounds and metallic dyes like Malachite Green. For protozoan complaints other than Amyloodinium/Velvet (see below), I suggest formalin baths... in transition... Including moving infested specimens afterwards to new settings. You'll want to monitor pH and ammonia... daily... See the bottle re the formalin... stock solutions are 37%... there are some guidelines for its use posted in books, on the Net... You want to do this few minute dip/bath with plenty of aeration present and with you in constant observation. You are in essence going to "burn" off the outside slime of the fish... and with it the encysted parasites. Moving the host fishes will leave the encysted, not-yet infective stages of parasites behind. Allowing systems to "go fallow" (sans hosts) for a month or more... perhaps with elevated temperature, lowered specific gravity... will expedite these resting stages die-off.

For Velvet, I endorse using Chloroquine diphosphate (an antimalarial medicine) at 5-10 mg/L for 10 days. Like copper, this compound is toxic to invertebrates and algae, and unlike copper, quite expensive.

Regarding hyposalinity treatments, garlic, "reef-safe" remedies... I am not a fan of such... And after responding to many situations over decades time with these fishes, can state categorically that although Scorpaeniforms are quite euryhaline, they're not easily cured of pathogenic disease through reduced salinity... that garlic (Allium sativum) is best used on pastas, and that reef-safe remedies that are efficacious and non-toxic don't (yet) exist.

Cloze:

Can't afford a Rhinopias (Me neither), don't have room for a full-sized Lionfish species? Looking for something really neat to spiff up your possibly small reef? Though rarely seen in the trade, this little Scorpaenid is worth looking for. It is highly interesting, colorful, easy-going... hardy to aquarium conditions, and always a conversation item.

The Waspfishes, Leaf Fish or Sailback Scorpionfishes, Subfamily Tetraroginae

The subfamily Tetraroginae contains eleven plus genera (*Ablabys, Amblyapistus, Centropogon, Cottpistus, Neocentropogon, Notesthes, Ocosia, Parcentropogon, Tetraroge, Vespicula*) of thirty five species. Very venomous. Mostly marine, with the Australian eastern coastal *Notesthes robusta* being able to be kept in hard, alkaline freshwater.

These fishes are very venomous... as their affiliation with the Scorpionfishes alludes to... Distinguished from this group by having their dorsal fins originate high on the head.

Ablabys taenionotus (Cuvier 1829), the Cockatoo Waspfish. Tropical West Pacific; Indonesia, Philippines, Australia. To six inches in length. Found on sand and mud bottoms. N. Sulawesi photos.

Hypodytes rubripinnis Temminck & Schlegel 1843. Northwest Pacific; Japan, Philippines. To four and a quarter inches in length. N. Sulawesi photo.

Paracentropogon longispinis (Cuvier 1829), Wispy Waspfish. To 8 cm. Indo-West Pacific; Thailand, Indonesia, Australia. Nocturnal for the most part. N. Sulawesi pic.

The Ghoulish Scorpion/Stonefishes of the Subfamily Choridactylinae (Inimicinae)

Subfamily Choridactyline (Inimicinae). Two genera, ten species. Occasionally imported and sold in the trade. Venomous and sedentary; preferring to hide under a mucky substrate with just their eyes showing.

Inimicus didactylus (Pallas 1769), the Bearded Ghoul. Indo-West Pacific; Thailand to Vanuatu, up to China. To eight and a half inches in length. Very venomous to the touch. N. Sulawesi.

Inimicus filamentosus Cuvier 1829, Two-Stick Stingfish, Red Sea Walkman... Western Indian Ocean; Red Sea, east Africa to the Maldives. To ten inches in length. A fish that really walks about... on its pelvic fin elements. This one strutting its stuff in the Red Sea.

The Deadly Fishes Called Stones: Family Scorpaenidae, Subfamily Synanceinae

Subfamily Synanceinae; the Stonefishes proper. Six genera, ten species

Synanceia horrida (Linnaeus 1766), the Estuarine Stonefish. Distinguished from the more common S. verrucosa by its much more elevated eyes. Aquarium photo.

Synanceia verrucosa Bloch & Schneider 1801, the Stonefish. Indo-Pacific; Red Sea, East Africa to French Polynesia. To sixteen inches in length. The celebrated rock-like pug-ugly Stonefish (there are others called by this name). World's most widely distributed stonefish and most venomous. Here in in the Red Sea, and S. Sulawesi

Orbicular Velvetfishes, Family Caracanthidae

Aka the Coral Crouchers, these little (to 7 cm.) fishes are found squeezed in between stony coral branches; are spiny/papillosa in appearance, laterally compressed themselves... eating small invertebrates. Most are reddish and white; and though not commonly seen in the trade, a few are at times offered to aquarists. They can live in captivity, given habitat and directed foods supply.

Caracanthus maculatus (Gray 1831), Spotted Coral Croucher. To two inches in length. Indo-Pacific; Indonesia to Polynesia. Lives amongst Pocilloporid and Acroporid coral branches. Wholesaler aquarium photo.

The Crocodilefishes, Family Platycephalidae

Family Platycephalidae, the Crocodilefishes or Flatheads. 18 genera of about 60 species.

Though all Platycephalids get too large for any but the most humongous hobbyist systems, some are sold into the trade on a regular basis. IF you get one, do your best to just feed it, rather than accelerating its growth by too frequent, too large offerings.

Cymbacephalus beauforti (Knapp 1973), Crocodilefish. Western Pacific. To 50 cm.

Papilloculiceps longiceps (Cuvier 1829), Tentacled or Carpet Flathead or Crocodilefish. To one meter in length. Western Indian Ocean; Red Sea, South Africa, Madagascar. The most common of nine species of Platycephalids in the Red Sea. Occasionally offered as a juvenile, but a real vacuum-cleaner feeder even when small. Red Sea and aquarium wholesaler pix.

Thysanophrys carbunculus (Valenciennes 1833), Papillose Flathead. To 40 cm. Lives in muddy, shallow habitats. N. Sulawesi image; Typical partly buried in sand and muck posture.

The Sculpins (Including "Freshwater Lionfishes"), Family Cottidae

Eleven families; 137 genera,   about 631 spp.

Family Cottidae, Sculpins

Sculpins occur in freshwater and marine habitats; most of the marine species used in our interest are caught by hobbyists themselves in tidepools in cool to cold climates; these have to be maintained in a chilled setting. The family includes the notorious "freshwater Lionfishes".

Sculpins are generally small (a few inches) in length; armor-encased, brownish in color, and hop along the bottom by way of their pectoral fins; using the tail only to spurt out of danger.

Scorpaenichthys marmoratus Girard 1854, the Cabazon. Northeastern Pacific coast; Alaska to Baja California (coldwater). To three feet in length in the wild. Found on rocky to sandy shores. Eat crabs, fish, and molluscs. Flesh very good to eat, but greenish roe are toxic.

Family Cyclopteridae; the Aptly Named Lumpfishes

More in the public aquarium domain, these comical, slow-moving fishes can be kept by home hobbyists; given appropriate sized chilled systems. Some do get big; and are very messy for coldwater fishes.

Cyclopterus lumpus Linnaeus 1758, Lumpsucker. Northwestern Atlantic. To 60 cm. Males smaller, reddish to purple in breeding color. Feeds on com jellies, medusae, small crustaceans, Polychaetes, jelly fish and small fishes. Aquarium pix.

Eumicrotremus orbis (Gunther 1861), the Pacific Spiny Lumpsucker. North Pacific; Japan to Washington. To five inches in length. At right: one showing the prominent ventral fin disk at the Birch Aquarium in San Diego, CA. USA. Below, juvenile female and male in captivity.

Scorpaeniform Wound Management for Aquarists

(Venomous, but Not Poisonous)

I'd wager that most aquarists and serious divers are aware that due to their tropical West Atlantic invasion, Lionfishes are potentially dangerous to touch… that some of their stout fin spines can deliver painful toxin along with mechanical injury. I'd further guess that there is an even larger group that knows these fishes to be delicious to consume; delectable even. But few dive-community people are knowledgeable regarding just how many Scorpion or "Mail-Cheeked" species of fishes there are; but they should be. Several of these are also painfully venomous; though quite a few can also be delightful food items.

Here I'll present the usual few examples of incidences of puncture and envenomation; how to avoid such, and a not-too exhaustive systematic review of Scorpionfishes I have encountered. You will be surprised at how many you too have met up with; and hopefully become more cautious in looking for them.

Scorpaeniform Fishes on Parade! A Review

All told there are 25 "Scorpionfish" families, of about 166 genera, comprising some 1,271 species. There are "a bunch" of "Scorpionfishes" to put it mildly. All have large heads bearing spiky processes, with most having large eyes and mouths to match... for the most these fishes are sedentary to slow moving, cryptically marked and camouflaged, serving for surprise attack to stalking fishes... many, but not all are venomous... with hollow dorsal fin spines that can inject (with mechanical pressure) powerful proteinaceous toxin... These stings HURT mechanically and chemically! For brevity's sake we'll only cover the groups whose members you're more likely to come upon.

Family Scorpaenidae, the Scorpionfishes and Rockfishes. 56 plus genera and 388 species.

Subfamily Scorpaeninae, Scorpionfishes and more. 15 plus genera with more than 150 species.

Iracundus signifer Jordan & Evermann 1903, the Decoy Scorpionfish. Has a marking above the largely transparent base of the anterior dorsal fin

Rhinopias frondosa (Gunther 1892), the Weedy Scorpionfish. Indo-Western Pacific; East coast of Africa to the Carolines, southern Japan. To 23 cm.

that resembles a small fish... that this species undulates as a lure. Indo-Pacific near the ends of reef slopes on sand and ledges. To five inches long. Hawai'i image at night.

in length.

Scorpaena plumieri plumieri Bloch 1769, the Spotted Scorpionfish. To eighteen inches in length. Western Atlantic: Massachusetts, northern Gulf of Mexico to southern Brazil, Ascension and St. Helena. Found sitting on rocky bottoms 5-55 meters of depth... ambushing fishes and crustaceans for food. Cozumel image.

Scorpaenopsis diabolus (Cuvier 1829), the False Scorpionfish. Common in shallow sandy, muck and rocky areas in the Indo-Pacific; Red Sea to Hawai'i, Micronesia, Australia. Here in Hawai'i.

Taenianotus triacanthus Lacepede 1802, the Leaf Scorpionfish. Indo-pan-Pacific. To four inches overall length. Usually found amongst reef rocks in an open setting, rocking like a falling leaf. Comes in browns, blacks, yellows, reds. Fiji, N. Sulawesi, and Hawai'i pix.

Subfamily Pteroinae: The Lionfishes, Turkeyfishes among many other common names. Five genera, 17 species.

Two of the nine species of Lionfishes, Pterois miles and P. volitans have become established in the tropical West Atlantic. *Pterois miles* (Bennett 1828), aka the Devil Firefish, natural range spans the Indian Ocean and Red Sea. To fourteen inches in length. Here in Egypt's Red Sea. *Pterois volitans* ("Tare-oh-ease vawl-it-tanz) (Linnaeus 1758),   lions span the color range of banded red to black against alternating creamy white. Yes, black and red volitans lions are the same species. Pacific Ocean; N. Australia, Japan, Marquesas, Polynesia's Australs. One in Cozumel.

Though they're labeled "Dwarf" lions for their diminutive sizes, the smaller Lionfish species are just as venomous. Here is shown the Hawaiian endemic, *Dendrochirus barberi* off of Kona, and a Shortfin, *D. brachypterus* in Mabul, Malaysia.

Subfamily Tetraroginae: Sailback Scorpionfishes or Waspfishes. Eleven genera of 35 species.

Ablabys taenionotus (Cuvier 1829), the Cockatoo Waspfish. Tropical West Pacific; Indonesia, Philippines, Australia. To six inches in length. Found on sand and mud bottoms. A couple photos to show some of the color diversity of this species. Raja Ampat and N. Sulawesi, Indonesia

Subfamily Choridactylinae (Inimicinae): Two genera, ten species. From browns, reds, whites to mottled in colors.

Inimicus didactylus (Pallas 1769), the Bearded Ghoul. Indo-West Pacific; Thailand to Vanuatu, up to China. To eight and a half inches in length. Very venomous to the touch. One scared up above the substrate in N. Sulawesi.

Subfamily Synanceinae, Stonefishes. Six genera, ten species. Very often go unseen, though present.

Synanceia verrucosa Bloch & Schneider 1801, the Stonefish. Indo-Pacific; Red Sea, East Africa to French Polynesia. To sixteen inches in length. The celebrated rock-like pug-ugly Stonefish (there are others called by this name). World's most widely distributed stonefish and most venomous. Here in S. Sulawesi.

Some Painful Meet-Up Examples:

Our dive-trip patriarch, JackM is a long-standing scuba adventurer having logged several hundred dives in dozens of countries around the world. His practice in demanding that our collection of dive friends agree on the "next" itinerary ahead of the coming one has helped us to stay on a schedule of live-aboard and resort experiences for decades. His one serious fault is a lack of caution underwater… a laxity in where his body is and a propensity for "touching things".

Some pertinent examples with Scorpionfishes have occurred while Jack and I have been out in N. Sulawesi in Indonesia, Sipadan in Malaysia and Taveuni in Fiji… all involving his apparent carelessness in setting his hands down on the bottom without careful observation. On just one dive in Lembeh Strait Jack touched down on a *Scorpaenopsis venosa* AND *S. diabolus*!

A Personal Petfish Odyssey:

On returning from living in Japan in the late sixties (father was a lifer in the Navy), I resumed working in the field of ornamental aquatics in Southern Cal. On one excursion to the Mecca of wholesalers in Los Angeles I was fortunate to make a sojourn enroute to "Doc" Adams place, Long Beach Aquarium. This location was incredible to me; thousands of not-plumbed together glass tanks for freshwater holding and "refrigerator linings" for marines. In my naiveté I reached into one of these had had a dead Pterois Lionfish floating at the surface… and got stung but good. The take home message here is that these fishes mode of injection of venom is purely mechanical… you and or they or both coming together to force venom from sacks near the base of fin spines… whether the poison-bearer is alive or no. So… even in death, watch how you handle them.

Prevention: Avoidance!

Forewarned is forearmed! And speaking about forearms; you've got to watch where your body is… and stay off the bottom; rocky, sandy or otherwise. Remember; these fishes rely on hiding in plain view, some under the muck and sand to avoid detection and act as ambush predators. Though some of the "above the bottom" species may seem to aggressively approach divers at times; the vast majority of sting incidents occur from hapless divers setting their hand, legs et al. right on the envenomizing fish. Be aware of your surroundings; look for these fishes. Some species are quite common within their distribution… just overlooked by divers.

Once Stung:

You'll definitely know if you've been poked… the mechanical injury itself is painful; and depending on just how hard you've pushed onto the animal, some venom may be forced into the wound. A sensation not unlike a social insect (bee, wasp…) sting is immediate, followed by a burning feeling, swelling and tenderness from the wound, spreading outward within minutes.

As with insect stings, reactions vary widely to Scorpionfish venom. Some folks report mild discomfort; others difficulty breathing, paralysis and delirium. IF you've been Envenomized, you should exit the water, inform others that you've been stung, and soak the punctured area ASAPractical with as warm freshwater as you can tolerate to denature the proteinaceous venom. Severe reaction, concerns call for immediate medical attention.

Fish hard-spine (anterior dorsal, anal fin) wounds are painful period; potentially leaving antigens in you whether there is venom involvement or not. The wound itself should be cleansed, dried and a topical anesthetic applied; followed by covering the area with a non-binding, light bandage.

Some folks have advocated, relate actual using of analgesics of various kinds, Benadryl… If you are partial, and not allergic to these compounds; they may grant you some pain relief.

Some good numbers to have on hand in addition to 911: National Poison Control Center at 1-800-222-1222. 911, DAN +1-919-684-9111

Bibliography/Further Reading:

http://www.fishbase.org/Summary/OrdersSummary.php?order=Scorpaeniformes

Howe, Jeffrey, Gerald Crow and Jay Hebert. 1988. The strange-eyed Scorpionfish, *Rhinopias xenops*, with comments on its Hawaiian distribution and aquariology. FAMA 9/88.

Nelson, Joseph S. 1994. Fishes of the World, 3rd ed. John Wiley & Sons, the World.